SELECTED POETRY BOOK VII

NEUTRINO SPINOR TRANSCENDENTAL COUNTERPOINT 21ST CENTURY POETRY

PAUL SHAPSHAK, PHD

authorHOUSE®

AuthorHouse™
1663 Liberty Drive
Bloomington, IN 47403
www.authorhouse.com
Phone: 833-262-8899

Published by AuthorHouse 07/14/2022

Library of Congress Control Number: 2022913579
ISBN: 978-1-6655-6539-4 (sc)
ISBN: 978-1-6655-6540-0 (e)

For my wife, Solveig

Ysein afelde aforth aliri derke derne luft shope swynke make
poraille glewmannes
--- Anonymous

Neutrino communications paint intergalactic wheels, wheels
besides wheels, or past wheels
--- Anonymous

Contents

PART I.   Pastoral...1
               Canzone 101...5
               Epigramme 101...6
               Canzone 150...7
               Epigramme 140...8
               Epigramme 150...9
               Canzone 155..10
               Epigramme 45 11
               Canzone 26 12
               Canzone 33 13
               Epigramme 41 14
PART II.   Mythology 15
               Epigramme 23 19
               Epigramme 44 20
PART III. Cosmology..21
               Canzone 67..25
               Canzone 35 26
               Epigramme 123..27
               Canzone 141..28
               Epigramme 179..29
               Canzone 172..30
               Canzone 112..31
               Canzone 153..32
               Canzone 203 33
PART IV. Theology 35
               Epigramme 102..38
               Canzoniere 201...39
               Canzone 49 40
               Epigramme 200 41
               Canzone 13..42
               Epigramme 14...43
               Canzone 15..44

Epigramme 17 45

PART V.   History...47

Canzone 22 50

Canzone 31...51

Epigramme 25...52

Canzone 44 53

Epigramme 53 54

Epigramme 54 55

EPIGRAMME 63..56

Epigramme 79...57

Canzone 39 58

Canzone 57 59

Canzone 61...60

Epigramme 47...61

Canzone 68 62

Canzone 58 63

Canzone 103...64

Epigrammaton 81 65

Canzonieri 17 66

Canzone 211...67

Epigramme 83 68

Epigramme 84 69

Canzone 83 70

Canzone 91 71

Epigramme 90 72

PART VI.   Social..73

Epigramme 91...77

Epigramme 47...78

Canzone 51...79

Canzone 52...80

Canzone 55 81

Epigramme 48 82

Canto d15...83

Canto f 84

Canto f3 85

PART VII.   Economics 87

Canzone 7 91

Canzone 9 92

Canzone 71...93

Canzone 31 94

Canzone 213...95

Canzone 83 96

Canzone 85 97

Epigramme 5 98

Canzone 97...99

Canto c 100

PART VIII. Health 101

Epigramme 13...103

Epigramme 99 104

Canto b 105

PART IX. Cybernetic Allegories................................107

Epigramme 31 111

Canzone 13...112

Epigramme 15...113

Epigramme 120 114

Canzone 16...115

Canzone 72 116

Epigramme 121 117

Canzone 202 118

Epigramme 107 119

Canzone 50 120

Epigramme 29 121

Epigramme 31 122

Canzone 63 123

Canzone f 124

Canzone j...125

Epigramme 33 126

Canzone 11...127

Epigramme 59 128

Epigramme 67...129

Epigramme 89 130

Canzone 19...131

Canzone 17...132

Epigramme 123..133

Epigramme 217..134

Epigramme 129..135

Epigramme 147..136

Canzone 19...137

Canzone 53 138

Epigramme 67...139

Canzone a 140

PART X. The Arts 141

Canzone 73...144

Canzone 79...145

Canto 41..146

Canzone 37...147

Canzone 57 148

Canzone 71... 149

Epigramme 73.. 150

Canzone 29 151

Canzone 23 152

Epigramme 37.. 153

Canzone 37.. 154

Epigramme 37.. 155

Canzone 79.. 156

Epigramme 23 157

Canzone 159.. 158

Canzone 93 159

List of Illustrations

Photograph 1.   Valley of a thousand hills 2

Photograph 2.   Kara 3

Photograph 3.   Drakensberg shield 4

Photograph 4.   Forest Idyls 16

Photograph 5.   Wrestling angel 17

Photograph 6.   Atropos Clotho Lacheris 18

Photograph 7.   Arthur Miller 22

Photograph 8.   Relativistic string theory 23

Photograph 9.   Neutrino intergalactic communication 24

Photograph 10. Abstract 6 36

Photograph 11. Ten 37

Photograph 12. President Harry S. Truman 48

Photograph 13. President George Washington 49

Photograph 14. kwa-Zulu Nduna Nkanei 74

Photograph 15. Poet Laureate Brendan Behan 75

Photograph 16. Dynamics 76

Photograph 17. Mahatma M. Gandhi 88

Photograph 18. Zero sum spinors 89

Photograph 19. John Nash equilibria 90

Photograph 20. Hans Egger 102

Photograph 21. Abstract 3 108

Photograph 22. Abstract 4 109

Photograph 23. Abstract 5 110

Photograph 24. Abstract 1 142

Photograph 25. Abstract 2 143

PART I

PASTORAL

Canzone 101

Pastoral place

Cantabile di molto

Summers' solstices wrest meadow
Air schlieren distances grove
Shaded wide perambulate
Pastures fences heightening
Hitherto ever sunlit shadowers
Lauded view outlook Laudate
Promontory collecting shadows expanse
Accords reap
Bayesian paradox
Rereadings *de capo*

Epigramme 101

Commentary

Allegretto cantabile

Short occasion un falter
Bent reed
Abate
Idiom column construct
Wane
Set temporal gloss esteem
Hesitate
Construe confluence
Vacillate
Wave
Valley

- Paul Shapshak, PhD -

Canzone 150

Spring Autumn

Allegro molto

'Twixt archangel
Addition autumnal-early freeze
Age banish
Ample banter
Alien bare
Drape
Time's aurora
Sphere

Epigramme 140

Design

Impetuoso

Agora bare
Allayed bargain

Angel baroque
Before blunt-scope
Beleaguer boundless
Unadorn
Unembellish

Epigramme 150

Desconfire

Allegretto a contendre

Cornucopia foison displicare
En table ennui chanson
Groves fueillage tranquillie
La folia en pais

Canzone 155

Exchequer

Cantabile

Betake bundle
Betwixt canonical
Bleak cheque
Bless'd care chide
Faces summer reflection
Lawn dandelion breeze staid

- Paul Shapshak, PhD -

Epigramme 45

Cobra

Impetuoso

Reticent
Inaudible
Doubt
Din
Quiet
Whisper
Cloak shield
Accord basic

Canzone 26

Jaguar

Allegro

Folly's reckoning providence
Province
Inane
Fate's fond trick
Faults hinder
Culpability forbidden force
Wildlife quills foreswear
Drab deterioration meagre
Caution fell abandoned
Deck forlorn demolish
Equivalents forsake structure

Canzone 33

Scissions

Andante cantabile

Sharp intergalactic
Sheaves formal
Shed snips
Shower surreptitious
Shun strengthen
Self-collected steel'd
Self-resemblance slice
Semblance neigh
Semblance song-lay

Epigramme 41

Pasture gyre kestrel

Vivace ma non troppo

Separable divergence
Discrete bifurcation
Separation genus echo
Assemblies' vineyard
Set dumbfounding
Seven stays folding disburse
Shade spent among

PART II

MYTHOLOGY

Epigramme 23

Counterview

Marcia moderato

Cunning counterpart
Deposition design
Disbarred debate
Debt determine

Epigramme 44

Device

Presto subito Allegro con moto

Dispersed expedient
Redoubts dishevel
Enmity dreaded
Envied dwell
Elder estuary
Follied antiquity
Despondent foreswore

PART III

COSMOLOGY

René Shapshak

Canzone 67

School

Allegro con brio

Planck De Broglie Schrodinger Dirac Maxwell
Born Heisenberg Jordan Einstein Feynman
New school
Quantum Field interactions Classical Action Lagrange integral extremum
Classics forms Heisenberg uncertain
Balmer quanta quads Hamiltonian
Principled Relativity
Quantum relativity

Canzone 35

Dyssymmetries

Allegro

Time-symmetric electromagnetism
Retardive advanced damping
Time's arrow
Maxwell-Minkowski-Wheeler-Feynman-Dirac
Field superimposition
Null-cone geodesic undistribute
Past-resolution future-absorb
Higgs falling into a black-hole
The rabbit lost watch
Rotation is just a rotation
Shrinking and radii cool heel

Epigramme 123

Siren

Allegro assai

Dare dark
Demise dispose
Disposition debt
Desert disorder
Derive dreary dream
Dread envy
Elder estuary
Disposition dispraise

Canzone 141

Siren

Allegro

Bessel LaGrange deadbolt siren
Thermodynamic random time
Radiation arrow retarded-advanced time
Cosmological time klaxon lea
Pythagoras vibrating em field
Strings strung strange
Waves prolapse
Shake bake walls bounce hither yon
Advance future retard regard
Reach hot cold

- Paul Shapshak, PhD -

Epigramme 179

Threaded Timed

Andante serioso

Forewarned wing
By fortune weight
Fate forearm
Providing providencial

Canzone 172

Travaille Paradigm

Allegro tempo giusto
Forza del con suspires

Poynting neutrino
Casimir anvil reap
Reaper
Lever momentum
Hammer
Hardly beset

Canzone 112

Hypergeometries

Prestissimo impetuoso

Sickle morning risen dawn opening
Scythe-riven
Sea-bound
Recolte revisit
Even keeled balanced roster
Remaining dread

Seal slow-even
Seep smile-fox
Self smile
Shadow stable
Shallow stain
Praise stand
Admire avowed

Canzone 153

Medusa Field

Allegro rubato

Medusa Field
Submerged
Emergent
Space time
Time call by gone
Present future time
Medusa Antimedusa
Antimonies exist
Gone by
Paradox
Higgs W Z sunk
Planet

Canzone 203

Fields

Lento ma non troppo

Medusa reflect
Bosonic star
Realmed incognito
Invisible

PART IV

THEOLOGY

René ShapShak

Epigramme 102

Epoch A

Vivace elegante

Contrapunctal invisibility
Inflectional Vach cyclic
Mantras five stage
Mme. Blavatsky cyclic gravitation
Surya Nada
Sveta Dvipa Svapna Svara
Panini agglutinative
Rule 3996
Yudhishthira vivasvat
Satyan nasti paro dhanah
Sila Dhanu
Akshara Adhyaya
Sloka Smriti
Udana Tula UdanaTattva

Canzoniere 201

Epoch B

Allegro a lentamente

Vajra Upeksha Upassruti
Vijnanamaya-kosa Vasudeva
Ahinsa Abhaya Avatara
Arupa Tohu Vavohu
Eka chakshu
Gupta Vidya Parampara
Jiva Hiranyagarbha Hansa vahana
Maha Maya Loka Kshetrajna Kshanti
Nagarjuna Nada
Paramatman Padma Nivritti
SamsaraSamadhi Sabda Ratna Ratri
Shanti Khechara Jnana
Advaita
Parasakti paratantra Phren
Prithivi tattva Pravritti
Aham Atma vidya Asrama
Dana

Canzone 49

Capstone

Allegro cantabile

Duteous dust erased
Dweller earth err'd
Erst Eden escape estuary field
Eternal elder evermore field
Fine firmament
Flair excel flame
Folk work dispel post haste
Hastened chasten chandelier quiet
Quote yoked brass braize
In brambles brazen
Humility unscorched
Policy dint
Device disperses debt
Disport disposition dispose
Flatter extant
Flaxen flight eye beam
Twixt plateaux kshetrajnya
Hone algebra

Epigramme 200

Descent

Allegretto

Despair
Stolen
Steeled despise
Debt's devise
Determine disparage detrimental
Dispel
Evocation filch'd evoked spoken
Yudithrustra
Evolved exceed
Exchequer buoyant
Flat expire express
Fleeting fair
Floss flourish
Mill *en passant*
Waterfall
Fair flora

Canzone 13

Lento tempo semplice

Subtle
Caveat embrace
Comprise
Clarion call
Decided proposition
Enhance arm-length winter dost decline
Debility decline dependence
Dominate endure shaded shadow
Merged no edges hedges nor prolegomenae
Not Stepped climb
Ad lib ration libation
Passing over cups' saucer
As if it were
Frail threads windy slope
Palatine thane degrees digressions

Epigramme 14

Apprenticed

Allegro moderato

Therefrom
No falseness
Flow
Nor false history
Fallow falter
Foist
Fold farrow
Date décor dateless
Desert dearth
Debar
Foiled farther
Folly

Canzone 15

Hypergeometries

Prestissimo impetuoso

Sickle morning rise dawn open
Scythe-riven
Sea-bound
Recolte revisit
Even keeled balanced roster
Remaining dread

Seal slow-even
Seep smile-fox
Self-smile
Shadow stable
Shallow stain
Praise stand
Admire avow

Epigramme 17

Secant

Allegro impetuoso

Shadow morning spur
Scope sins evanesced risen sun
Scope-blunt riven sketch
Scorn skill
Scythe skilled
Scythe sky
Skill
Scythe fêted

PART V

HISTORY

Canzone 22

True Dividend

Vivace

Truth creator right safe
Happiness prudent security
Assent governor sufferance
Providence appropriation
Establish
Charter magnanimity justice
Providence
Undivided
Divide

Canzone 31

Commons

Grave con brio deciso

Tranquility welfare advice consent concurrence trust opinion necessary
Consideration measures continuance attained secure accommodate
Relinquish compensation commiseration commons balance Intervention accord

Epigramme 25

Casuitroso cantabele

Obviate improvise embellish
Consequence obfuscates indicate
Confluent concurs concatenate
Synopsis suspiration spiritu conspiritu
El Segundo grande
Conflagrate

Canzone 44

Vivace moderato

Salubriously sole solitary from jot dot haven good growth
Grammarcy
Blend light
Light
Lit
Confluence

Epigramme 53

Allegretto

Remained mode iota timeless
Time & again

Epigramme 54

Contraindication

Allegro assai

Ingrain
Duality dualism dual twin twofold
Empower impede straight-jacket
Supply demand intersection curves
Consequence quince pomegranate

EPIGRAMME 63

Concatenate

Allegro moderato

Conscript draftee enrollment entourage reclaim recluse
Recuse loose cannon outsider anchorite eremite ascetic solitary
Conquest defeat subjugation overthrow rout capture upheaval

- Paul Shapshak, PhD -

Epigramme 79

Scant Scat

Allegretto

Reign sands	time's sail winch
Sardonic part	salutation spent
Sancted sparse	salubrious avow
Saturate deluge	salve slate
Ensconce	rumormontage unguent
Yet tea	scone silent
Distillate scope	quintessence sink
Recolte riven shade	encouragement delimited rejected
Shade spirit fray	embarked
Spilling ointments	splashed Autumn
Alluvial shaded	shadowed spoils
Spreading	spalled spoiled
Recounted	recoltes
Redeemed	stints
Tells	sands
Tolled	hillocks

Canzone 39

Dis-Inquisition discussed

Allegretto

Decorate folly
Decrepit debate fate
Daunt delegate
Discourse retributor
Deserve departure day
Depart days
Deposition providence
Deprive retributory design
Debarred despair deliberated

Canzone 57

Contiguous speculation

Allegro inverse

Transience dissemble mortgag'd steep
Legate
Assent
Invention mountain mortal lid
Front
Mountaintop's lour obdurate
Advance
Needful limit
Accent
Muse outspoken voice
Stepped steps

Canzone 61

Ordinate

A cappella

Judgment
Halter
Harangue happier keen ken
Dial judgement
Steering steerage stark stir
Kept kindred kingdom
Harvest blloms
Thousands swallows by-cliffs land-fall
Haste lair heart-inflaming laughs
Hem lawful
Hence

- Paul Shapshak, PhD -

Epigramme 47

Tire

Allegro contento

Attired sound cymbal
Work alter lanl fetch
Helm veer
Gyre stars reprobate ne'er
Cast lots wear vulture gyre
Guy drawn ware

Canzone 68

Adagietto ma non troppo

Anodyne
Good tiding
Tinges dawn beset
Furrowed brow
Cling marmoset
Flung bolas
Immovable steadfast

Canzone 58

Steps

Impetuoso a la breve

Caught steadfast
Drum embody sound afoot shaded
Fast recline dust aloof
Unique step sound arrest alit
Descended trim
Quotae

Canzone 103

Jonglesse M. de France

Largo tempo comodo

Lais laoidh
Breton
Chevrefoile
Espurgatoire
Jongleure
Loreine
Lorraine
M. de France
Plantagenet
Trefoile
Ywain
Green knight-errant
Skirted
Tabletop circumnavigated
Orbits

Epigrammaton 81

Ex abstentia

con spiritu

Glum
Glib
Glubb
Par square
In two

There
Absent

Deck disconsolate
Old city charm
Ingresses long
Far
Wide
Views
From wall
Wall to

Canzonieri 17

Ab abstentia

Gusto con pacerera

Escom house
Another time
Constant consonant continent

Visiting visitors' callers lauded
Step steppings steps

Canzone 211

Des de France et Villon

Largo alla tempo a comodo

Domain de France constant
Teem brought align
Villon conclave tread compose
Restitution rancor affine space
Tomorrow's fault dread tranced
Causative yesterday contain

Epigramme 83

Forensic

Adagio a temperamente

Stunned silence
Game afoot
Awry
Conglomerate
Beast burden
Disquiet daunt dissolution
Familiar disposal dents branch
Weave
Woven
Woof

- Paul Shapshak, PhD -

Epigramme 84

Moirai

Lo stesso tempo

Spindle thread
Separate
Retrograde' rethreaded
Retread
Before
Clio Mnemosyne
Beyond
Lachesis Clotho Atropos
Apart

Canzone 83

Coinage

En marche assai

Lai Breton
Villon F
d'Histoire
d'Anjou C
Duc d'Orlean C
de Coincy G
de Dargies G
de Machaut G
Li Vinier G
de France M
Le Chancellor P
De Vitry P
Herier T
Henri deuxieme
de Troyes C

Canzone 91

Ballade Petite

Impetuoso

N'estoit qui a qui
Riens de bon conseil
Apres de la fontaine
Paour de cheoir
Assayed Villon de bonheur
Des benois anges
Besoin l'art de memoire

Epigramme 90

Profile Transference

Allegro rotundo

Ail more

Alder	Myrtle
Angel	Appellee
Apricot	Beech
Blackberry	Boat shield
Bridge	Brig
Brusque	Cad goddeu
Cater fefynedd	Cedar
Chestnut	Clout
Elm	Woodbine gourse
Willow	Wight
Tree	Spruce
Roosts	Poplar
Pine	Pear
Grape Peach	Oak
Lyre	Holly
Height	Hawk
Apple	Harply
Harp	Gwydion

Fern

- Paul Shapshak, PhD -

PART VI

SOCIAL

Epigramme 91

Mills

Presto ma non troppo

Abound
Isospin spun
Twisters off-hand
Thrive
Prosper
Flourish
Fixed oscillation isospin

Epigramme 47

Zenith

Allegretto en marchant

Rampart Babylon's Babel over
Reached above
Jericho seared psychology
Deprived
Plain cities lakeside
Last year single thing
Psychiatry
Distinct entity
Done for congruent's more

Canzone 51

Mention

Elementale adagio

Ensconced outsource obscurity prey
Word loss pernaud naught
Line locked neutral neutrino abandoned
Remake neutral heavy remarked reap
Alpha muse time
Lofty newfound neglect luster
Loss o'rexpress omega lone patina
Ninefold line-bare nature lustrous
Lour'st obfuscate loud
Oblation glint abeyance

Canzone 52

Appreciativeness

A priori a cappella

Lay-song hence rehearse mist herein
Lease lest rehearing hibiscus
Rising snow plough
Mentor lent
Leaven leaves modern
Happier ken
Bracket moment leese
Lees barrel examine
Mortal lenient
Leisure lent mortal tenant
Broad inflection time
Pericarp capacious cantilevel
Spacious selectrin surface magenta

- Paul Shapshak, PhD -

Canzone 55

Counterpart

Grave ma non tropo

Complex
Supplement
Component
Receptor
Stable surface
Complex
Proper dins roll
Complex
For other days

Epigramme 48

Attended

Vivace

Temperate forlorn
Fiber-bundle temperate relinquish
Gestalt onwards memory fortune
Gloat providence
Fortune gilded
Baroque guild
Gilded-hope providence

- Paul Shapshak, PhD -

Canto d15

Distributed divisors

Concordia cantabile

Stat stem
Terse terms yesteryear
Year
Year
Reckon whereof
Wild while
Tides by bytes present
Plaster
Pronounced pronunciation
Year

Canto f

Divisors distributed

Concordia andantino

Stat stemmed
Carrier
Wave
Well-contend
Wend
Wending
West-gate
Tree
Thematic
Theme
Vocal
Themes
Thence
Where-through
Wrinkle

Canto f3

Distributed divisors

Concordia allegro

Stat stem
Wherefore wrinkle wreath
Whither willful

Wrang whilst whisper
Stem wisp
Wherefrom reefs reside probabilities

PART VII

ECONOMICS

René ShabShak

Canzone 7

Elektra

Allegro con spirito

Bright Tunguska
      Krakatoa
            Etna
                Thera
Day night
Haply pumice quartz electrum
Diamonds rubies sapphires
Scorched record
Connote crisp
Ensconce sojourn

Canzone 9

Hydroponics

Allegro con vivo
Day return
Reform expends tuned salaries brace
Crucial interjection
Hydras whirl stream

Canzone 71

Salubrious

Canzone

Allegro concordia

Caesar
Cato
Publius

Canzone 31

Respect

Canzone

Allegro moderato

Hamilton
Jefferson
Madison
Jay

Canzone 213

Amalgamate

Presto crescendo

Crucial conjunct
Interject
Found
Advantage
Anticipate
Paucity amalgamate
Amalgamate
Prudence
Confluence
Hydra
Stream

Canzone 83

Specific Widespread

Adagio grazioso

Strict qualm wayside embankment fear harvest
Stentorian trellis flow guard
Across
Stepped pools unseen quiescent
Voyeur vox steeped
Stippled canvas dread
Vastly redeem dreamt
Gerund part remark retrograde

Canzone 85

Turn

Lento placido

Ere
Turned complete strung
Systematic gain bygone
Forgone iota grains rain
Springs span Spring felicity
Travel concatenation self-same
Grasped gratuitous snatch
Syzygy synod multifactor
Compound design
Meant touch rasp flat drape
Diagrammed hue tinge

Epigramme 5

Remark

Lento subito

Tender
Delay
Droned
Reschedule
Meaning assembled
Self-poise
Secure
Meanwhile
Everywhere

Canzone 97

Leopardi

Allegretto lentamente

Plenty embellishment
Conversant lechatelierited
Crystal binded
Headlong-gait conduit
Discerned fluted agate
Columnatededly
Fox-beam veneer
Likeness obduratedly fragile
Expressionless frail flicker
Glamour frailly
Syzygy
Frailty glint frantic frenzy
Gleamed guileless defenselessness
Assured gloats exult glimmer

Canto c

Dealt considerata

Allegro ma non troppo

Suffice
Suede suave
Swayed substantial
Syzygy
Question

Strewn write thrum
Constituent accorded

Subtraction t'aint
Tale tallied

PART VIII

HEALTH

Epigramme 13

Complement

Simplice a marche

Footpath's twain
Diverge wander
Digress confin
Divagated congressed assert
Combined tort refrain
Brief sophist calamined redundant
Pathways reconscribe

Epigramme 99

Provençal

Vivace

En provence perdue du temps
Lest fall leaves wintry coat
Firs apparent
Ostensible departed mile
Dispense develop
Wind sound door
Betoken ground appropriation
Approach broach

- Paul Shapshak, PhD -

Canto b

Dealt factors

Allegretto

Photons' migrations
Time begins extant wind-up time contemporaneous
From
Galleries' room by room
From
To
Towards
Tantamount
Toured
Rested

Strung-sympathy style

Strewn resilient wrought
Subjunctive sentient
Substance

Undull'd substance

Teacher

PART IX

CYBERNETIC ALLEGORIES

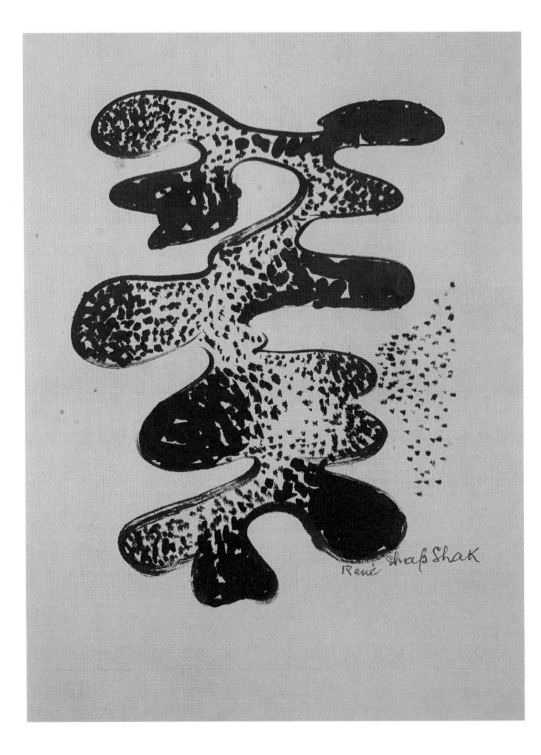

René ShapShak

3½ Inches

Epigramme 31

Jericho

Allegro vivace

Distinctly entity
Tenacious
Indigent
Current brocade
Woven
Psychiatry
By no cloth
Design

Canzone 13

Embark

Tempo a tempo

Seaside astral charismat
Sidereal litany legend
Feature register
Clan recitation
Alike semblance
Clan afar flung recollect
Relate
Provision
Entendres

Epigramme 15

La place Piazza

Tempo a tempo

Reminiscences
Preceding resemblance
Proceedings
Semblance remembrance possession
Past time
Time future
Indifferent interval
Gauge invariance
Tenements tasseled tamed grew
Oak fir maple pine
Contemporaneous
Clangor legend
Claymore existent

Epigramme 120

Board Paneled

Tempo interlocutor

Offering embers alight
Determine
Submissioned
Blossoms
Recognize
Cuchulainn Ferdiad
Fomorians
Faculty embers
Endowed
Cinder ash coal
Cath Maige Tuireadh
Tuatha De Danann
Char seared autumn
Leaves reddened beads
Charm charisma
Ornament
Lebor Gabala Erenn
Distinguish
Ablaze branch
Roost discerns
Dagda
Morrigan brim ample
Flourish
Nemain Macha Badb
Tain Bo Cualinge
Syzygies glazed
Galaxies inter concatenate
Time bent spent recorded threads

- Paul Shapshak, PhD -

Canzone 16

Arcane

Tempo allegro

Steadfast endure
Craftsman prompt
Dominion province
Lug spear
Lugdunum
Lughnasadh
Resolute apt stand
Dominion
Domain

Canzone 72

Demarcate

Lentemente

Brigid
Aibell
Aine
Macha
Eriu
Foretelling
Fortuitous preamble prompt
Presume
Epona cavalry
Nuada Airgetlam sovereign liege
Goibniu forge
Dian Cecht syzygy
Manannan mac Lir marine
Extrapolate chance explanation
Swift kiln analytic

- Paul Shapshak, PhD -

Epigramme 121

Capstone

Allegro cantabile

Duteous dust erased
Dweller earth err'd
First Eden orchard escape
Estuary field
Eternal elder evermore fields
Fine firmament
Flair excel flame
Device disperses disposition debts
Disport disposition dispossesses
Flatter extant
Flaxen flight eyebeams
Fixed aloft between

Canzone 202

Descent

Allegretto

Despair-stolen despised debts devise
Determine disparage detrimental dispel
Evocation filch'd evoked spoken Yudithrustra
Evolved exceed
Exchequer buoyant
Expired express flat
Fleeting fair
Floss flourish
Fall
Fair flora

- Paul Shapshak, PhD -

Epigramme 107

Apprenticed

Allegro moderato

No falseness flow
Nor false-history
Uncultivate
Falter far
Fold farrow
Date décor dateless
Desert dearths debar
Foiled farther folly

Canzone 50

Inquisitions

Allegretto

Decorate folly
Decrepit fate
Daunt delegate
Daunt retributory
Deserve departure day
Depart days
Deposition fate
Deprive design
Debarred despair debate

Epigramme 29

Zenith

Allegretto en marchant

Rampart Babylon's Babel over-reach
Jericho seared psychology deprive
Plain cities lakeside
Last year single thing
Psychiatry
Distinct entity
Indigent current

Epigramme 31

Andante ma non tanto

By river
Day
Daunting flow

By air
Path
Slumber
Current flow profile

Canzone 63

Larghetto

Beneath sea
Lake view
Ocean sway
Rear mountain
Aloft sky-height

Canzone f

Larghetto

Season
Creek breakdown
Arcane consultant
Stern fell
Uphill firmament elevation

Canzone j

Gaelic Canzone

Larghetto

Camhrail tir theach
Aidhbheis aidhbhse
Aigealaim aigean
Bratog breac caor
Tuathail ceart
Dealan
Dealbhach dealbh
Dorcha dorchuighim
Liathraim liathran life
Measana loch
Muin cheann
Oscardhacht priomh uachtaran
Reimheas

Epigramme 33

Impetuoso a la breve

Encircle disk
Anterior after
Flaxen echo
Parallel
Deliberated
Deliberate
Cautious thought

- Paul Shapshak, PhD -

Canzone 11

Larghetto

Oceanic light
Agile
Bright frame
Dexterous
Taught shallow
Anger in salubrious
Patience
Decent
Grotto belief
Skilled
Bas-reliefs
Sculpture
Music
Eisteddfod
Bring together
All things
Insubstantial
Universal
Slight
Figure

Epigramme 59

Gaelic Epigramme

Andante sostenuto

Beacht ceard
Tiachair
Clachan imrim
Imsheachain
Iolchroidheacht
Tairngim tairngire
Tairseacha
Bealach beannuightheacht
Ruadh bhuidhe
Fuaimneach ionntsanhla
Machtnoir toileamail
Toirbheart

Epigramme 67

Cobra

Andante serioso

Silencio hisses
Quietened
Quiet
Clamor
Din
Deadened
Pandemonium
Whisper

Epigramme 89

Unique Cobra Shibboleths

Allegro vivace

Idiosyncratic
Soph
Eccentric
Sophistry

- Paul Shapshak, PhD -

Canzone 19

Gaelic Canzone

Vivace

Briocht
Fhaobhrach
Neamh oidis tanag
Aidhbheis aigeantach
Foluthach
Geal gean
Iomchaol
Lamhach
Seolta tana
Teann taobhuighim slainteamhail
Tennaireacht
Slainteamhacht
Tualang
Caidheamhail
Uaimh uaim cheangal
Cliste
Breacaireacht
Briocht
Eisteddfod
Cead thosach ceann
Crion cuirim
Neamh thabhacht
Neamh thruaillidheacht
Ullidheach
Rud beag
Scruigin
Seanga chorp
Seanga chruth

Canzone 17

Allegro poco crescendo ritardando

Suborn tear
Subsist
Tender
Thematic

Tear stubborn persuad'd thieved
Tender constellation
Stellar
Extra dire essentially
Expell'd

Epigramme 123

Allegretto

Substance dull'd
Affluence
Subtraction theme
Substance theta
Sueded themes
Supposed thine
Thereafter
Suborn teacher
Sullen
Thereby sullied
Sultry therefrom
Summer's flower
Thereof
Suffic'd
Thence

Epigramme 217

Prospects

Allegro Impetuoso

Spread magnolia leaves
Stole surprised enveloped muddy time
Weary mid-day trolls' sunbeams
Searchers
Where-through
Strains arraigned trains straight-forward
Strange arrows marked time signs pull-back
Stratified push-forwards
Weather-beaten windvanes
Vapors vapid morning becomes electric shadows
Winds swell'd rest reclined double-beamed
Thrivers divers diners 66 highways denoted subscribed
Dissed tired triremes rhymed desultories
Danced trophies light trophic millipedants mauled loans
Clawed clarions castanets claret clarinets

- Paul Shapshak, PhD -

Epigramme 129

Under radar

Allegretto a pacitiero

Disc intense disparage
Ridicule
Elision midst intend
Shapes outlines slant
Patchworks
Degrees grade
Grim grey indispose
Pieties

Epigramme 147

Cryptic ravens

Allegro serioso

Reign

       sardonic

             sail hoist

Sardonic

             salutations

Sated

       salute

             saturate, salve

Scandal

       salve

             scone

Silent

       scope

             sink

Scope

       sins

             scope-blunt

Sketch

       scorn

             skill

Scythe

       skill

             sky

- Paul Shapshak, PhD -

Canzone 19

Shadow Jaguar

Allegretto mysterioso

Scythe

        sland'red

                scythe, slander

Scythe-hammer

        sea-bound

                sloth

Seal

        slow-even

                seep

Smile-fox

        Self

                smiles

Self-resemblance

        smote

                semblance

Snicker

        resemblance

                remembrance

Song-lay

        separable

                sonorous

Separate

        Sort

                unfeigned

Canzone 53

Shaded shepherd

Vivace spirito

Separation
        sounds
Sessions
        sour
                set
Speechless
        Sevenfold
                spent
Shade
        spent
                spirit
Spoil
        shaded
Shadow
        spread
                dispersed

- Paul Shapshak, PhD -

Epigramme 67

Panther leopardi

Largo

Shadow

        spur

            stable

Shallow

        stain

            stall

Sharp

        stalled

            star

Sheaves

        state

            shed

Shower

        stealth

            shun

Steel

Canzone a

Dealt Divisors

Allegro

Crease forte
Scattered string harmonic
Overtone spinor
Spindle overtone
Wrought yore harness
Tinted share glass
Oscillating seigniorial mirror spinorial
Gambols gimbals neutrino steer
Unfaltered
Gambol beams light
Gambata midst gauntlet
Red-shift
Lambda second place
Twix't place wave diadem
Ancien time undue tined
Kindle alternate finds

PART X

THE ARTS

Canzone 73

Pass Reflect Momentum

Sotto voce

Point

Uncaught fleet thought reflect

Brief sojourn between adjuncts

Ephemeral accessory remanded ardor

Evanesce confabulant brief halt

Moment rumor visit

Profound synonym wedge Clifford algebra

Transition deliberant pause move break

Sagacious promontory considerant

Argument

- Paul Shapshak, PhD -

Canzone 79

De capo

Allegretto constrained

Hassle happy-go-lucky endorse

Slap-hooey

Retort repeat

Well-founded substantiates

Accountability hurled eloquence

Peninsula outcropped respites

Restitution cape resumed

Repositioned revisited

Canto 41

GAELIC CANZONE

Allegro ma non troppo

Aon seolta ca formaluidhe
Toit bladh cadhain cearnach gloine
Earc ear ghabhail
Easpartain eibhleog
Fosclaim
Fras aereach iadhadh muig
Scor seabhcoir tascoir
Leagmhalaim
Teannta tearma ti tim
Tim aidhbheis aistear
Bicmin cablaim deanasach
Deigh mhillte
Dine do dine
Mor ghradhmhar
Mor luaigheacht
Bileogach duilleogach
Dilleog bhaidhte
Eis

- Paul Shapshak, PhD -

Canzone 37

Volume Cavalcades

Allegro ma non troppo

Conveyed works

Scinter'd glass fragment

Diffraction

Light shut darkness

Sections conical tasks set

Time ocean journey

Bound'd labor Egypt

'Til days by day

Belabor day arduous leaves

Ledgers leases

Day leaves goneby

Canzone 57

Cantor Ardor

A la breve

Guide impetuous gild importun'd
Cull gull impression-pity guilt
Lame iron
Interchange
Scythe
Hence long
Amalgamations
Ago
Egypt coalesces
Scythe

 - Paul Shapshak, PhD -

Canzone 71

Coming going

Andante moderato con spiritu

Adjust stage frame
Recommend cite
Egypt deep
Not for a moment forgot
Quoth authors cited
Time frame
Betelgeuse signal
Aleph centauri centurion
Arrived
Afta what
Mention
Time frame
Field left
Consequent

Epigramme 73

Theoretical Mists allocates

Allegretto resorgimento

Travel idea
Traverse
Foot stanza emphasis
Parallel transferences
Dominate
Prominences
Proceeds
Non-abelian
Growth
Common altruïsm
Solicitous exception
Broadcast approached
Broached blockade
Impediment stanced stencil
Staunched Recolte refrain
Dim fundamental
Dominant vague
Quelling quiet stratagem
Fact paradisial
Fiction paradisical
Psychiatric qualms question
Concession

- Paul Shapshak, PhD -

Canzone 29

Gone Remained

Andante moderato con spiritu

Frame time adjust
What afta time
After arrived
Signal Betelgeuse
Recommend
Aleph centauri
Commended time
Again field
Timed frame
Principles stand
Time framed
Principle

Canzone 23

Catwalk

Andante moderato tempo semplice

Word secludes
Question
Pose clued-up
Decide decline
Assura

Epigramme 37

Invigurato andante

Walk byway
Paired posts
Primed multiplied resonance
Summed isospin spins
Spinors
Decide

Canzone 37

Ascension

Allegretto cantabile

'twixt a'day Archangel
Epigenetics
Area beauteous aecia
Before beguiling begun
Blunt-scope perplex pledge books
Take classic separate under veil
Confabulate confine
Affirm
Confound congruent
Fit compatible

- Paul Shapshak, PhD -

Epigramme 37

Assumption

Allegro moderato

Architecture 'twixt a'day awry
Areas beguiled
Book confabulate classic confounded

Canzone 79

Decline declination

Allegro vivace

Conquest abhorrent cloaked
Day confined before substantial attachment
Disorientate pledge blunt-scope disinclined
Depot irritable author fastened
Confession beguiles night day
Archangel hid midst cloven herd
Before balanced day night firm
Curtains knight known
Discovered prime

Epigramme 23

Connote

Allegro vivace

Drill brush
Dank dim
Donate ample overtone gauge
Device superposition superpose

Canzone 159

Sumer summer

Allegro sotte voce

Branch watercourse insubstantial ascent
Parallelogram intersection irrigate tone
Contradict fate concatenate ardor
Collide course deliver dreamt hypnot kip
Converge disparate reveried afternoon
Sun primary star banqueted slumbered
Plain plethora sighted sojourned
Six hundred standards
Completed time's pillar
Rough dreamt consigner
Tree descent simple sighter
Motivate slight disaggregate
Disparate remedy deregulates combine
Recline commune remain see hypnotize distance
Marshal magnitude
Compel consequent undine
Agate basalt

- Paul Shapshak, PhD -

Canzone 93

Impend

Andante moderato con spiritu

Alter interval threshold
Egypt
Citation
Phase set
Quote
Brought again
Betelgeuse beckon
Appear concern
Regarding
Rommel
Left Egypt
Period edge
Marble granite

Printed in the United States
by Baker & Taylor Publisher Services